TOOLS FOR TEACHERS

- **ATOS:** 0.9
- **GRL:** C
- **WORD COUNT:** 30

- **CURRICULUM CONNECTIONS:**
  animals, habitats

Skills to Teach

- **HIGH-FREQUENCY WORDS:** and, are, have, in, mom, the, these, they
- **CONTENT WORDS:** baby, black, follow, forest, kits, live, play, skunks, spray, stinky, stripes, white
- **PUNCTUATION:** exclamation points, periods
- **WORD STUDY:** long /a/, spelled ay (play, spray); long /e/, spelled y (stinky); long /o/, spelled ow (follow); multisyllable words (baby, follow, forest, stinky)
- **TEXT TYPE:** information report

Before Reading Activities

- Read the title and give a simple statement of the main idea.
- Have students "walk" though the book and talk about what they see in the pictures.
- Introduce new vocabulary by having students predict the first letter and locate the word in the text.
- Discuss any unfamiliar concepts that are in the text.

After Reading Activities

Ask children to think of the ways in which skunk kits are unique. They can spray a smelly substance as a defense. Explain that defenses are special skills animals have to protect themselves. Do they know any other animals that have different defenses? Why might they need them? Ask children to draw a picture of a different animal using a special defense.

Tadpole Books are published by Jump!, 5357 Penn Avenue South, Minneapolis, MN 55419, www.jumplibrary.com

Copyright ©2019 Jump. International copyright reserved in all countries. No part of this book may be reproduced in any form without written permission from the publisher.

Editor: Jenna Trnka **Designer:** Anna Peterson

Photo Credits: Matthijs Kuijpers/Alamy, cover; Eric Isselee/Shutterstock, 1; Papilio/Alamy, 2–3, 16tm; KenCanning/iStock, KenCanning/iStock; JayPierstorff/Shutterstock, 6–7; Betty4240/iStock, 8–9, 16br; age fotostock/SuperStock, 10–11 (foreground); Zack Frank/Shutterstock, 10–11 (background), 16tl; Holly Kuchera/Dreamstime, 12–13, 16bl; critterbiz, 14–15, 16bm.

Library of Congress Cataloging-in-Publication Data
Names: Nilsen, Genevieve, author.
Title: Skunk kits / by Genevieve Nilsen.
Description: Minneapolis, MN : Jump!, Inc., (2018) | Series: Forest babies
Identifiers: LCCN 2017061706 (print) | LCCN 2018001189 (ebook) | ISBN 9781624969751 (ebook) | ISBN 9781624969737 (hardcover : alk. paper) | ISBN 9781624969744 (pbk.)
Subjects: LCSH: Skunks—Infancy—Juvenile literature.
Classification: LCC QL737.C248 (ebook) | LCC QL737.C248 N55 2018 (print) | DDC 599.76/81392—dc23
LC record available at https://lccn.loc.gov/2017061706

FOREST BABIES

SKUNK KITS

by Genevieve Nilsen

TABLE OF CONTENTS

tadpole books

SKUNK KITS

These are kits.

They are baby skunks.

mom

They follow mom.

black ···▶

white

They are white and black.

stripe

They have stripes.

They live in the forest.

They play.

They spray! Stinky!

WORDS TO KNOW

forest   kits   mom

play   spray   stripes

INDEX